The Hilarious Side of Funny

True Anecdotes to Laugh Your Ass Off

By Dean Aulichme

TABLE OF CONTENTS and DISCONTENTS

"One Dad, One Tube, Several Pills, and Two Gallons of Gas"
"One Moron Brother"
"One Mom, One Dad"

Preface

"Truth is stranger than fiction." Mark Twain

I wrote these true stories because for years I've been sharing them and getting lots of laughs with my poker buddies, while raking in chips.

All stories are 100 percent true will not cause drowsiness, those with asthma may need a break between stories. Let each story sink in one at a time. My wife doesn't find any of this funny, which means I'm onto something. She won't have a problem when cashing in checks if this book hits it big. Most stories, to protect your wardrobe, have a DGF Rating (defined below) so as to pre-emptively protect you from ruining your nice pants form the ensuing laughter, I hope. No *live* animals or humans were abused while writing this book.

DGF Rating=Dick Grabbing Factor Rating is how hard you have to squeeze your Johnson so as to not wet your pants. DGF Rating, 10 being the tightest grab. For women, I'm not sure how that all works still, so you'll have to adjust accordingly.

I had some really hilarious kicker lines, but couldn't use them due to laws prohibiting "trademark tarnishment." Also, there are about four times the amount of slang words for vagina as there are for penis, which should piss my wife off even more than a cold speculum.

Note: If you have flashbacks or déjà vu of a woman sticking a tube up your ass, keep reading.

About the cover: My wife stopped opening deliveries after she opened up a package containing an enema bulb. As a result of this, I get the strangest pop ups now on web sites for adult diapers and male urinal sheaths.

"One Five-Year-Old Kid, One Toilet Bowl, One Vanishing Toothbrush"

DGF: 9.5, but zero if you are a family member. Yes, Mom, forty-five years later, it was me that did the vanishing toothbrush trick.

Our toilet starting clogging for no apparent reason. When I was five, I thought it was undignified to use my fingers to wipe my ass, even with toilet paper. I decided that if I wrapped the paper around a toothbrush, my fingers wouldn't have to go anywhere near my asshole. Of course, I wouldn't use my own toothbrush, I was a smart five-year old. I must have dropped the kid-patented toothbrush ass wiper in the bowl and decided not to get my fingers dirty and flushed away. My Dad had to replace the toilet. My Brother was curious about what the cause of the clog was so he whacked away at it with a sledge hammer until it cracked in half. The family was carefully watching "the reveal", or "prestige" portion of the trick. Inside the guts of the toilet was a toothbrush with soiled toilet paper neatly wrapped around it. I, of course, stayed cool, *really* cool. My family stood there in disbelief with a bewildered look of disgust contemplating that someone was using their toothbrush to wipe their ass. Had someone asked me directly if it was me, that would have been easy, I would have blamed it on a cousin. I think I had over 100 of them. And no, I never married one, you wouldn't have either.

"One Electric Fence, One Giant Piss for Mankind"

DGF rating: 9.1

I was ten years old picking strawberries on my grandparent's large property. I had to take a wicked piss. I was a good half mile away from their house so I decided to piss near something, like a dog. It turns out I was standing near an area that had a fence. I whipped out my pickle and I started taking a leak. Next thing you know I get pounded by what seems like a very large rock slamming into my left heel. I look down to see nothing near my foot so I'm thinking one of my idiot Brothers is throwing rocks at me. I look around and there is no one around. Still pissing, I gaze down at the fence I realize that there's a wire attached. It turns out that I had been pissing on an electric fence. What made the electric shock so amazing is that it pulsates so the piss would've had to be touching the wire at the exact time the electric current was pulsating. The wicked pain was the shock of the grounding effect in which the current traveled through my cock and shocked the living hell out of my heel. Thank goodness just the heel. Luckily, a placebo like effect has made me feel as though this shock gave me special powers sort of like when Spiderman got bit by spider. For years, I wanted to tell my friends that I was "Stud Man", but decided not to until writing this book.

"One Garbage Man, One Baby Poop Cocktail Supreme"

DGF: 10 if you were there, 0 if you were the garbage man

My wife and I are sitting around one day and we had garbage pickup coming. The garbage truck pulled up at the normal time. What came next seemed surreal. I heard the loudest scream that a man could possibly make. "EEEEOOWWW!" I thought for sure that the driver had ran over his partner's foot. I grabbed the phone thinking that I would have to call 911.
My wife and I were in different rooms and we both ran to the window to see what the brouhaha was all about. It turns out the garbage man was, for the first time, experiencing a foulness way beyond normal garbage man standards. This baby poop cocktail supreme also included lobster carcass and maggots that had been boiling in a tightly sealed garbage can during a three day 98° summer heat wave. This guy was having an out of body experience, literally. You could see this guy hacking up all sorts of bodily fluids from both his mouth and nose like he was performing a self-exorcism.

"One Embalmer's Assistant, One Bottle of Vinegar"

DGF: 9, 0 if you were the Embalmer's Assistant

The last thing in the world you want to be when you are a kid is the makeshift embalmer's assistant. Let's jump right into this. Back in the 1940s, poor people in Canada that could not afford a proper burial with formaldehyde. Option B was to buy a cocktail for a home brewed viewing. A proper poor man's viewing would last approximately a week because it would take that long for people to get there. As luck would have it, my Father's gig as embalmer's assistant was to be the person that would hold the funnel inside the dead person's mouth while watching his Father pour vinegar into the deceased corpse. If this wasn't bad enough, they would need to return every few days to add more vinegar as the smell would get worse over time. I hope they used Balsamic.
I figure that my Father had gone through this incredibly negative experience on numerous occasions. The irony of it all is that my Father went on to become a church organist and performed at over 1000 funerals. For fun, one year I packaged up a bottle of vinegar and a funnel for a Christmas gift, of course, it came from Santa. If asked directly, I would have said it must have been from a cousin. Can you put embalmer's assistant on your resume?

"One One Minute Steak"

DGF: 5.5

Back in my youth, our family diet mainly consisted of minute steak and potatoes. The steak was like eating a baseball glove with butter. No salad, no vegetables, nothing that would help your bowel system move in any way. How was I supposed to know that dropping a monster bi-weekly was not normal? It's not like I was going to ask my teacher, "Hey, Sister Mary, is it normal to be taking a, how do I say it, forgive me, you know, the number two bi-weekly?" In those days, you'd get whacked in the head and given detention for two weeks. Today, they would thank you for flushing.

"Sixty Pounds of Meat"

DGF: 2.3 on a good day

Deceptively, your intestines have crevices that can hold in meat.
Apparently, Elvis died with 60 pounds of meat stuck in him, I heard this on some infomercial for some colon cleansing concoction. It must be true, right? How did they get that info on Elvis?

"One Guy, One Grande Tennis Can"

DGF: 10+, 0 for my Mother

One day my Mother got really pissed off at me and told me to go to my room. "Under no circumstance, let me highlight the word *no*, circumstances are you to leave your room!" About an hour into my mini prison sentence, I had to take my bi-weekly monster dump consisting of baseball gloves and butter. So now my bowels are killing me and, of course, I can't leave the room "for any reason." Now I did have a balcony outside my window, but that would look strange seeing a monster deuce billy club drop from the second floor on US Route 1. I looked around my room to find something, anything that I can drop this deuce in, period. Luckily, I played tennis and lo and behold, I had a brand new unopened three-ball can of tennis balls. Reluctantly, as these were pricey balls, I open the tennis can and let the three balls out. I proceeded to squat myself to get a gravity assist dropping the bi-weekly baseball gloves directly into the can. The tricky part was that while this monster is exiting my body, like an exorcist shit, I had to piss at the same time. I had to be *extra* careful as the inside rim of a tennis can has a really sharp edge that would create a self-inflicted John Wayne Bobbit type scenario (those of you who are younger will definitely want to look this up *right away*, see you in a few minutes). Welcome back. Luckily for me I was fairly skillful with everything making my acrobatic style evacuation as sparkling as a whistle, no toothbrush required here, this baby was delivered clean.

Like an idiot, I left the tennis can on my dresser, almost completely full, cap on of course. When my Mother came to let me out she did a double take. She said, "What is that?!" I, of course, feeling proud of my skillful delivery admitted to my Mother that I dropped a deuce of a lifetime in the tennis can. Watch, some idiot will YouTube step-by-step directions on how to do this. Start eating minute steaks two weeks in advance.

"One Colon, Several Cubic Feet of Plasma"

There are four states of matter: solid, liquid, gas, and plasma. After years of eating baseball gloves with butter my system was irregular to say the least. I must have had some good broccoli or cabbage at a cousin's house, and since I hadn't dumped in like, forever, the gas was coming out like you read about. These were plasma steamers which had plenty of shelf life and they went on for hours. They felt like they were microwaved before exiting the chute. I could've supplied enough plasma to fill a storeroom of TV's. I had to go lay in bed. I decided to get back at my Brother by keeping the door and window closed to our shared room. Soon it was bedtime. After minutes of gagging and being pissed off, my Brother somehow got used to the smell after some time. He and I decided to wrangle my Dad to come into the room, and upon entering his arms immediately began flailing. This was immediately followed by, "I walked into a wall of pure shit" with his thick French-Canadian accent.

"One Movie Theatre, One Big Cup of Soda"

DGF: 0, but if you try this, then 10

The one and *only* time I decided to splurge and buy
myself the super duper sized soda that cost a small
fortune was at a movie theatre. I sat down and as
there were no cup holders, placed the 5-gallon drink
on the floor. While getting my popcorn situated, I
kicked over the super-sized soda and the cover came
off. People for 20 rows ahead of me where looking at
their feet as a river of soda was washing their shoes.
I'm confident that people had sticky shoes for weeks,
like leaving a cheap peep show. I, of course, was
squeaky clean and was pissed off about the loss of five
bucks. Never again, well, maybe a few more times.

"One Poker Game, No Bathroom, Poker Chips and Finger Food"

DGF: 5.5, zero for the players

I got invited to a decades long Friday night poker game in a garage with a nice spread of finger foods and beer. Eventually, I have to go to the bathroom so I ask the host where the bathroom is. He said, "Go anywhere outside." I then told him I had to drop a deuce and he said, "Go to my neighbor's back yard." Upon returning I ask if there is a sink to wash my hands or a bottle of hand sanitizer and, as expected, the answer was "No." As I'm playing my next hand, I watch in disgust as guys are eating finger foods and shuffling their poker chips. I can't figure out why ten guys can afford a $200 buy in, $300 of food and beer, but can't spring for a $2 bottle of hand sanitizer. I hope these guys aren't Eucharistic ministers.

"The Stage Past Fart Confidence"

DGF: 6, would have been 9 without any laws prohibiting trademark defamation

One morning while eating bacon and eggs at my Brother's house, he comes into the kitchen and tells his then wife, "A forearm with some deer pellets." I make the mistake of asking what he means and he proceeds to tell me that he was describing what his BM looked like. I take it they were way past fart confidence stage. Later in the day on our way to a gun shooting range, his wife has to get a cup of coffee. Upon entering the car, she says "A billy club with nubs on the end." I then had to drop a real monster at the shooting range and we all got a hefty waft of it on the way out. In the car, I said "Tricolored, like a salad with bacon." His wife looked at me with disgust. I said, "What did you expect, a candy bar with a truffle?"

"One Pair of Pliers, Some Hillbilly Dentistry, No Anesthesia"

DGF: 10 for some people, zero if you're the poor bastard

My Father used to work at a logging camp. Every few days a local doctor would stop by to give care to anyone who needed stitches or whatever. The whatever is where it gets interesting. Occasionally someone would need a tooth banged out. Because the doctor was not a dentist he or she would have to perform hillbilly dentistry. It would take several people to pull out a huge molar. One person was needed to hold down the person's head with a towel at the end of the table. The doctor would have to use pliers the pop out the tooth. A third person would be necessary the supply towels and booze. My Father distinctly remembers a very harsh back and forth motion with pliers until you heard that very distinct cracking sound a molar makes when extracted from the head. I would have parlayed this into a novelty act and charged admission.

"One Flute, One Man"

Yes, this *will* go where few men have gone before, I
promise

DGF: 10, yes definitely 10

A band student had a flute that really smelled, like,
you know. This student went up to their band teacher
and said that her flute smelled like shit. This rookie
teacher asked to verify this by taking a good whiff,
and when his eyes watered, believed every word. The
same thing happened a few weeks later to a different
flute player. Imagine how uncomfortable this young
teacher would feel having to approach his principal
and discuss this sick fetish. Amazingly, the school
setup a sting of some kind and caught the guy. Turns
out it was the night custodian putting the flute head
piece up his man hole.
Imagine the laughs his boss had when writing the
letter of reprimand. "You are hereby fired for sticking
a flute up your anus." How else could you write this
up? Then a meeting with union people and
administrators take place. Could you imagine? I
would have to jump under a table and hold my pecker
and nose while I was laughing my own nuts off.
Coincidentally, he is a regular at the poker game that
doesn't use hand sanitizer, I swear it, pinky swear.
This is the kind of reality TV we need in the world.
Not watching people starve to death or have marital
disputes.

"Two Guys, One Car"

DGF: 9.5, zero for the Two Guys

Apparently, on occasion, two people can get locked up. Yes, you read that accurately. Friends of mine were working in an emergency room and in the parking lot they could see two guys walking through the parking lot one directly behind the other with a bed sheet covering themselves up. It looked like a two-man conga line. The only thing missing was the song "Common Baby do the Conga." Upon entering the hospital emergency room the two gentlemen made their way to the counter and the front man said, "Hi, we're like, stuck."
What is truly remarkable is that they drove themselves to the emergency room. What I would like to know is who was maneuvering the cars pedals? Was it the top man or the bottom man? If they got pulled over, who's at fault? I would also like to know whose insurance provider had to pay? Is this a pre-existing condition? Could you imagine what the phone call between insurance companies sounded like? "Your guy is at fault because it was stuck in him." "No, your guy is at fault because he didn't use lube." Thank goodness that the act didn't take place while standing at the center of the four corner states, causing even more confusion. I can hear it now, lawyers haggling over who's ass was in Utah.

"One Sleazebag, One Homeless Guy"

I know a landlord that had a rental. The rental wasn't supposed to have pets, but as expected, the asshole had a dog anyway. This sleazebag tenant figured out the system and knew he could get a free ride of six months without paying rent before the cops came in to boot his ass out. Well this dirt bag was a special kind of dirt bag in that he knew how to play the system for more time. When the cops came to boot the tenant out, he was sheltering a homeless guy and as a result of this, he could milk an extra two weeks out of the rental. Finally, the cops get him and his junk out. To assess the damage, landlords typically show up with a flashlight as the tenant always has the power cut off. Upon descending into the basement, a horrific smell took over his olfactory nerves, and as he puts it, "I could see the damn floor moving." Turns out the dirt bag let his dog die in the basement and the floor movement was the maggots moving upon seeing the flashlight.

"One Woman, Many Sponges"

DGF rating: 7 or 8, for the woman it ranges from 1-6.99

One day at the ER a woman was being sponge bathed. Turns out, to her delight, they found an old sandwich and a remote control. The woman, without embarrassment, said, "Oh, that's were those things went." I wonder if the TV changed to higher channels if she moved to her left and lower when she moved right?

"One Cop, One Village"

Someone I know was a cop in a big city. Once, well probably more than once, a guy had a cock ring that got stuck and wouldn't come off. He was totally whacked, in more ways than one. He called the wrong rescue service to come help him out. When the cop opened the door, there it was, his swollen braciole hanging in the wind with a cock ring stuck bad at the base of his shaft. Cop says, "Why the hell did you call *us*?!" Response "Ehn, eh, hep me." Turns out the fire department has a special saw for the occasion. I hope the EMT doesn't drink too much coffee during the shift, otherwise that shaft would be in real trouble.

"One Guy, One Rubber Doll"

DGF: 8.2

What can I say about a guy who owns a rubber love doll? Recently, the news had a guy that owned his own doll that he would take out on shopping sprees, dress her up, have tea with her, the works.
Pros: she quiet, non-judgmental, has only good hair days, stays clean shaven all over, you can use her in the HOV lane, and you can fit her in the overhead compartment.
Cons: only if you have a latex allergy

"One Chinese Parrot, One Cheater, some Moo Shu"

DGF: 10, unless you're the parrot

A guy was cheating on his wife in China. When in the act, he would say his lovers name. The house pet, a parrot, began repeating the lovers name and the wife caught on. Imagine having been outed by your parrot? Not a regular parrot, but one that speaks Chinese. He probably fed her the bird, but called it General Tso's Parrot and some Moo Shu.

"One Guy, One Cup"

I know a guy that had to get a semen analysis. He goes to the clinic and they put him in the "secret masturbation room." It isn't so secretive as it's near the andrology lab, you may as well put the name "Jack Mehoff" on the door. The lab worker walked him into the room and said, "Make sure you lock the door behind me." Great advice. Imaging if someone walked in? There were three old porno magazines in a folder all in surprisingly mint condition. A woman must have been in charge of this room. The room was very cold and the lights were bright. No couch, no videos, no posters, nothing, except for the collection cup. I guess his HMO didn't include the extras. It sounds worse than a shitty peep show for homeless people. To make matters worse, there was no Wi-Fi. Had a man been in charge of this room, it would have at the very least have had one of those pens that a naked lady shows up when you turn it upside down. You'd need a third hand as one would be used to hold then pen and another to hold the cup.

"One Garbage Strike"

DGF: 6, 0 if you're the sucker

A friend of mine had a garbage collection strike in his town. Getting rid of your garbage was a real pain in the ass. He came up with a great way to get rid of garbage. Around Christmas time you would take all of your garbage and put it in a big box or two and wrap it up in Christmas paper. Then you would drive to a mall and leave your car unlocked.

"One Dog Sitter"

DGF: 10, depending on how you look at it

A married couple in a big city needed a dog sitter for a week. They told the dog sitter that under no circumstances would they accept a phone call during their vacation. Even if their building were to burn down they still would not want a phone call. A few days into the dog sitting experience, the dog unfortunately passed away. The girl who was dog sitting panicked and called a local vet for advice. The vet had a great idea and told her to bring the dog to them so that they could put the dog on ice for a proper burial. To transport the dog to the veterinarian's office, she decided to put the dog in a suitcase. While hailing a cab on street level some jackass decided to steal the suitcase.

"One Guy, One Lake, and Two Nurses on their Knees"

DGF: 8.5, 0 for Guy, -1 for the Nurses

This story has a happy ending with two nurses on their knees. A man fell through the ice and drowned in an ice-cold lake. Talk about shrinkage. They brought him into the hospital and the doctors tried everything to revive him. Nothing worked as there were no vital signs of any kind. They had to call the time of death and put the toe tag on him. When the staff was waiting around the nurse's station for the morgue to pick him up, they were very sad. After about 15 minutes the nurse's station got a beep from the dead man's room. They gave each other a puzzled look. They quickly went to the room only to discover the once allegedly dead man sitting on the corner of the bed and toe tag hanging and asked, "Where am I?" Before the guy had time to notice, they distracted him by taking his pulse while two nurses were on their knees cutting off the toe tag.

"One guy, One ED Pill"

If your pocket flute doesn't function properly, no problem, they have a pill for that. If God is watching us as some experiment gone wrong, he or she will wonder how we can find a cure for flaccidity of the phallus and not cancer. Some guy I know had to get his ED pecker pill. I wonder if there a test to verify that you're lying? Do they attach a probe on your yogurt dispenser to see if it moves when a hot blond enters the room? One day this guy ran out of pills and needed more. The big weekend was here. He calls his doctor and begs to get his prescription filled. Luckily, a male doctor understands and fills in the prescription immediately. This guy gets denied at the pharmacy because his doctor sent the prescription to two pharmacies to guarantee his phone would stop ringing. We can't catch deadbeat dads, but we can temporarily stall a man from getting his ED pills. My wife is pissed because you have to wait 24 hours to get female birth control pills. For men, no blond, no probe, no wait, just lies and some extra red tape.

"One Guy, One Woman, Two Rashes"

DGF: 4.88

A woman goes out to a bar one night with her friends. A man from across the bar buys her a drink which she gladly accepts and he comes over to talk to her. She figures, why not? She decides to have a one night stand.
A few days later she develops a painful rash around her mouth and snatch so she goes to the doctor. After the doctor examines her, he has a shocked look on his face. He proceeds to tell her that the last time he saw that kind of rash was in medical school twenty years earlier when he was working with cadavers. It just so happens that the guy she hooked up with was a mortician.

"One Dad, One Tube, Several Pills, and Two Gallons of Gas"

DGF: 10, For Mom and Dad zero

My Father had surgery on an *internal* organ. Some pain meds can give you really bad gas. My Dad was suffering from unspeakable gas pain. He needed some big-time relief. It didn't help that he was a two pack a day smoker who never exercised, ate lots of cheese, drank wine, and ate baseball gloves with butter.

Conveniently, one of our neighbors was a nurse. My Mother decided to call her and ask if there was anything she could do. I can just imagine what this conversation sounded like? "Hey Mrs. Doe, can you come over and help my husband out, he's got incredible post-surgical gas pain, you know, the wicked pill farting type?" As luck would have it, she said, "I'll bring my things, I know exactly what to do." The nurse then entered my parents' bedroom and proceeded to ask my Dad to go on all fours. If this isn't strange enough, he then looks between his legs and watches while this woman inserted a long tube up his ass. After several minutes of gas spewing out of the tube, there was both relief and wicked rank odors. I sincerely hope that my Mother did not offer to return the favor. What kind of parting gift do you give a woman that performed a tubal-up-ass-gas-relief-a-thon? Did they wave hello to each other on the street after this with a big smile? Is this considered a bonding experience? You'd get hit by lightning before you could find a local nurse willing to come over and perform this feat. Isn't there a Hippocratic oath that says, "Thou shall not make personal house calls, particularly involving sticking a tube up another man's ass in his bedroom while his wife is watching?"

"One Moron Brother"

DGF: 8.1,

My oldest Brother did some really stupid stuff, things I learned *not* to do.
Once he decided to ride a bike with his eyes closed, ran into a pickup, got stitches. On another occasion, he went shooting a rifle with a big scope and, of course, his head was too close to the scope and the gun kicked back. Another round of stitches. I, of course, don't have any stitches.
I went on a million hunting and fishing trips with him. I would either get eaten alive by 100,000 mosquitos or freeze to death, while never having caught anything. Once I fell into a stocked trout pond that he illegally brought me to and the owner showed up with his dog and a shotgun. I was running way faster than they do in the scary movies.
To get him back, like an idiot, he would like to try to impress me so I would taunt him to eat 20 fig cookies at once or 3 hamburgers. Watching him gag and choke with food halfway out of his mouth was priceless. Of course, I would take pictures. I didn't mind as much when my Mom would bitch at him for being, you know, him. I loved those days when Mom would get the roll of film developed and it would come in the mail and he wasn't home. Listening to her howl about him being a moron was better than Christmas morning.
After years of eating baseball gloves with butter, he went on to work full time at a fast food chain, eating

their greasy food for 5 years. As expected, he had to get an upper GI series. Apparently, they have this contraption that you sit in and it rolls you upside down. They stick a tube up your ass and fill you up with some x-ray juice. They then have to plug you up with a cork, string included. Of course, they bring you back to your recovery room and, as luck would have it, some hot nurse would tell you to go into the extra small echo chamber bathroom and pull the string. This shart-a-thon would last for a good five minutes. Luckily, you get this procedure done in the hospital instead of at home. Oh, and ironically my Brother has a genius IQ, no joke, and is now a college professor. He's still a moron.

"One Mom, One Dad"

Hi Mom, if I offended you in any way, oops, sorry about that. Oh, and if you want to make it up to me for the tennis can, you can give me your condo someday. Thanks, Dad for making me laugh my ass off. You had a way about your humor, even when you took your fake teeth out, and brushed them, hopefully with an untampered toothbrush.

After purchasing tubing for the front cover to go along with the "One Tube" story, I got an email with the subject line, "Did your new vinyl tubing blow your mind?" I would have to say at this point no, but my Brother has a nurse that lives next door to him. Maybe I'll send him the tube and ask him after his next surgery.

Thank you for reading this book! I hope the humor made you laugh as much as I did when my family discovered that I was wiping my ass with toilet paper around their toothbrushes. I'll admit it also made me remember what the best of times are, and how they happen when you least expect it. Please tell a friend about this book, I really do have a toilet to fix.

One last thing, when Dad died, the doctors harvested his eyes and they found a recipient. I just read an article that said that the eyes are actually part of the brain. If you're the recipient of my Dad's eyes, now you know why you are having flashbacks or déjà vu of a woman sticking a tube up your ass.

Reviews

"Son, I can't believe you outed the family like this. To think a very small number of people will read that our neighbor shoved a tube up your Fathers' ass!"

    - Mrs. Aulichme, mother of author

"Son, I was the church organist, you really had to share that story?"

    - Mr. Aulichme, father of author

"Thanks, little Brother, did you have to tell everyone that I'm a moron!"

    - Professor Aulichme, brother of author, moron

"A cold speculum? Really?"

    - Mrs. Aulichme, wife of author

"Daddy, what does DGF mean?"

    - Offspring of author

Made in the USA
Lexington, KY
21 December 2017